Writing at Work

STRATEGIES FOR TODAY'S
COWORKERS, CLIENTS, AND CUSTOMERS

NATASHA TERK

Wiw Write It Well
Business writing that gets results.

Corporations, professional associations, and other organizations may be eligible for special discounts on bulk quantities of Write It Well books and training courses. For more information, call (510) 868-3322, or email us at info@writeitwell.com.

© 2016 by Write It Well

Publisher: Write It Well
PO Box 13098
Oakland, CA 94661

(510) 868-3322

info@writeitwell.com

writeitwell.com
adcomdesigns.com

Author: Natasha Terk
Editor: Christopher Disman
Past contributors: Janis Fisher Chan and Diane Lutovich

ISBN: 978-0-9824471-8-5
eISBN: 978-1-5323-2488-8

To order this book, visit writeitwell.com and online booksellers.

Our publications include the following books, e-books, and e-learning modules from The Write It Well Series on Business Communication:

- *Essential Grammar*: Brush up on grammar, punctuation, and usage details that help you project a professional image

- *Land the Job*: Tailor your resume and cover letter to a specific organization's hiring needs

- *Effective Email*: Improve the quality and reduce the quantity of your job-related email

- *Professional Writing Skills*: Plan, draft, and send any document at all to match any professional purpose (for readers with time for more detailed techniques than you find in *Writing at Work*)

- *Develop and Deliver Effective Presentations*: Plan, rehearse, and deliver a presentation on any professional topic

- *Reports, Proposals, and Procedures*: Draft multisection, high-stakes business documents

- *Writing Performance Reviews*: Keep performance documentation clear, specific, and appropriate for today's workplace

Write It Well offers a variety of customized on-site and online training courses in half-day, full-day, and multi-day lengths:

- Writing Resumes and Cover Letters

- Effective Email

- Writing at Work

- Professional Writing Skills

- Technical Writing

- Marketing and Social Media Writing

- Superintendent Writing Skills

- Management Communication Skills

- Global Teamwork and Meeting Skills

- Presentation Skills

- Writing Performance Reviews

CONTENTS

CONTENTS

CONTENTS

INTRODUCTION

The importance of writing skills

We surveyed our clients and showed them imaginary email samples with document-planning or sentence-level errors. About 85 percent of these client readers told us they would have formed a less positive impression of the email senders.

Readers form an impression of you based on how you write. That's why communication skills are crucial for managers, business owners, and people who want to get ahead in their own careers.

Skills you can refine here and now

This is a compact refresher course for people who'd like to brush up on their writing skills for today's workplace. The course presents strategies to communicate effectively with customers, clients, and coworkers, across devices and platforms.

Many people find it hard to keep up with how quickly the business world changes. Maybe you find it hard to keep track of the sheer range of ways to share business messages, from traditional email to the latest cloud-based collaboration tool.

Most of us have been responsible for sending out half-baked emails, ambiguous questions, and unclear project updates. Our digital environment raises the stakes since we receive more written messages, and more people can see what we write.

This course includes pointers for your own writing, and it can also prepare you to coach coworkers on their writing skills. Careless, unclear writing can waste time and cause frustration. With some carefulness and tact, you may be able to help people avoid those outcomes.

When you complete this course, you'll be ready to cover all these bases:

- Identify your readers' concerns and their questions about your topic
- Identify your primary purpose and your main point
- Organize a message logically:
  - Write an effective subject line
  - Write effective salutations, opening paragraphs, and closings
  - Organize information in list form without burying it in long paragraphs
- Use clear, concise, appropriate language
- Present a professional image by avoiding common errors

Ways to prepare and practice

Think of any kind of document you need to write for work — preferably, a typical writing challenge from your own job:

- An email, a letter, or a short report could be a good choice
- It should be longer than a text message, but shorter than four pages

Take some notes on who you'll send this message to, what results you'll need, and what details you'll include. You'll leave the workshop with a draft you can type up and send.

Ineffective, unprofessional writing

Business writing is different from personal and academic writing: each business message should start with a clearly spelled-out purpose. Look through the following email and ask yourself what you'd think if you were one of the readers.

> **FROM:** **Department Manager Kurt Lee**
> **TO:** **Customer Service Staff**
> **SUBJECT:** **Email Response**
>
> We are very fortunate to be in an industry that is expanding. However, there is no reason to be complacent since our competition is working hard to catch up. We must continue to optimize our opportunities.
>
> Again, I want to thank you and say keep up the good work. Customer service will continue to be important and we have received a larger number of emails than in prior months, and some of the questions about the product are difficult to answer and I understand that it takes some time to figure out who is the right salesperson for each of the clients. I have heard complaints, however, from customers, that they got an automated response from the system but didn't hear back from a sales rep for almost a week. That is: unacceptable because our policy is different. I followed up on a couple of these complaints and it looks like our team has been slow to get the messages to the right sales rep; you know, I know that there is a lot going on, but we have a high work load and we need to be as productive as possible!!! If you can't contact the write rep, you need to: write or come to talk to me about it because we need to improve these numbers (our customer service guidelines state that anyone who writes should get a personalized message within 24 hours, so let me know if thats a problem). I would like to thank each of you for the extra effort that you have expended as a result of the heavy work load.
>
> Sincerely,
>
> Kurt

Here are three questions about the email:

1. Can you identify the writer's main point? (Write it down.)

2. Did you have to reread the message to understand what the writer's trying to say?

3. What's your image of the writer?

Effective business writing

Wasting people's time is an easy way to lose their readiness to cooperate. Busy readers need to grasp a message quickly, and they have other important tasks to get back to.

Efficient, effective business writing meets three criteria:

- States the main point clearly and makes sure readers notice it
- Leaves out unnecessary information while it organizes all necessary information in a logical sequence
- Uses correct, clear, concise language that all readers can follow easily

The following four chapters will give you strategies for mastering each of these challenges for any document at all that you need to write for work. Appendix B includes resources to go into further depth for more specialized forms of business writing, such as work email, proposals, or performance reviews.

1   PLAN FOR SUCCESS IN FIVE STEPS

In this chapter, you'll review strategies to keep the writing process efficient and effective for everyone. Planning a message makes it much more likely that you'll get the right results.

Writing is an asymmetrical process: it should take more time to write a business message than to read one. Always start writing by identifying what your readers care about, focusing on how your information or a course of action will benefit them.

Your coworkers, clients, and customers are probably drowning in a sea of both their own work and potential distractions. Even if a reader only skims what you write, you're more likely to get their attention by highlighting their interests, needs, and concerns. Strategic planning on your part can result in messages that catch busy readers' attention, provide them with exactly the information they need, and motivate them to help you out.

Different documents call for different writing tactics, but all business writing should start with planning. You can plan pretty much any written message by following these five planning steps:

1. Identify what your readers care about
2. Identify your primary purpose in writing
3. Identify your main point
4. Answer your readers' questions
5. Organize your information

Step 1. Identify what your readers care about

Sales and marketing teams learn as much as they can about their buyers' interests. As consultants who specialize in communication skills, we've learned over the decades that the more you know about your audience, the better you become at getting their attention.

Successful business writers put themselves in their readers' shoes and identify why particular readers will care about the message. Your writing improves when you figure out your readers' motivations and figure out what ideas will catch their attention.

Here are some sample questions to help you figure out what your readers need to see in your writing.

- **WHAT ARE THEIR BUSINESS PRIORITIES?** You'll catch your readers' attention more easily when you focus on what *they* want to get done in their own workdays.

- **WHAT'S THEIR MOTIVATION TO HELP YOU?** A cordial tone can help motivate readers who don't have a built-in reason to spend time on you — say, a successful project from last year.

- **COULD YOUR MESSAGE MAKE READERS UNCOMFORTABLE OR TRIGGER A DISAGREEMENT?** Careful planning can help you show respect for others, maintain your self-respect, and keep the focus on the mutual benefits of doing business with one another.

- **HOW FAMILIAR ARE THEY WITH YOUR TOPIC?** Your job may have made you familiar with specialty terms that your readers won't recognize. In those cases, use plain English or explain any new terms.

- **IS THERE ANY KIND OF SALES PITCH IN WHAT YOU'RE WRITING?** If so, it's especially important to spell out what your readers stand to gain.

EXERCISE 1.1

Think of the document you're planning for your own job. Identify how one or more readers will benefit from spending time on your message — for instance, by earning your gratitude, avoiding a risk, or saving money.

How will your message build on your readers' interests, their informational needs, and their own business goals?

YOUR ANSWER:

If you don't know anything about your readers, how could you try to learn more?

YOUR ANSWER:

Step 2. Identify your primary purpose in writing

Step 2 builds on Step 1. Keep your readers and their needs and interests in mind as you identify a primary purpose for your message.

Think of this step as a Venn diagram. Your primary purpose maps out the overlap between two things: what your readers need to see plus your own reason for writing.

Try to steer your purpose in only one of two directions:

- Your primary purpose is <u>either</u> to pass on key information (**WRITING TO INFORM**)
- <u>Or</u> it's to persuade readers to take action (**WRITING TO PERSUADE**)

Business readers need clear, focused text. Any message becomes much more streamlined when you try to apply either / or thinking about whether your primary purpose is to inform or to persuade.

Writing to inform

When your primary purpose is to inform, you're writing only to pass on information. What the readers do with that information is up to them. In these cases, you don't make any requests, and you're not asking readers to take any action beyond paying attention.

Here are some sample, informative topics that people regularly send other people at work:

- I'm announcing a preset agenda for a meeting
- I'm describing an attached file
- I'm passing on relevant information
- I'm answering a question you asked
- I'm announcing a course of action I've decided to take

Writing to persuade

When you ask readers to take a specific action, you're writing to persuade, and not just to inform. Even a single request in a long message can change its primary purpose.

Here are some actions that people regularly request at work:

- Please prepare to discuss this topic for an upcoming meeting
- Please send me a file
- Please answer this question
- Please approve a course of action I want to take

Of course, all business writers need to include information in order to persuade readers to take action. But in persuasive writing, the information is secondary. If you add information to a persuasive request, the information should explain why your readers should take action or should expand on what you'd like them to do.

Chapter 2 includes tips on how to structure a persuasive message so that even a single, minor request won't get lost in a multipage document that's full of information. But for now, remember that you can always step back and plan *two* clear, separate messages in cases like those. An informative message several pages long can come first, followed up by a quick persuasive request. Splitting up a message like that can represent excellent message planning based on clear recognition of more than one purpose for writing.

EXERCISE 1.2

Read this email and decide whether the writer's primary purpose is to persuade the reader to do something, or to inform the reader about facts she needs to know.

FROM: Eileen
TO: Jasmine
SUBJECT: Three-shift coverage in Processing Dept.

For the last several weeks, the Processing Dept. has worked with three-shift coverage. Employees have covered the day shift and swing shift while a temporary employee has covered the night shift. The third shift was covered on a trial basis and is scheduled to end this week. This arrangement has been satisfactory, and we should continue it.

Write your main point here: I THINK THE PURPOSE IS TO ...

Here's a revised version of the email. Can you identify Eileen's primary purpose now?

> **FROM:**   **Eileen**
> **TO:**   **Jasmine**
> **SUBJECT:**   **Three-shift coverage in Processing Dept.**
>
> I recommend that we continue three-shift coverage since it's working well. Please let me know tomorrow what you decide.
>
> We've met all our deadlines and made the most efficient use of employees' time. That's because we've had company employees cover the day and swing shifts and also because we hired a temporary employee for the night shift.
>
> Thanks for letting me know your decision,
>
> Eileen

I THINK THE PURPOSE IS TO ...

EXERCISE 1.3

Read this email and identify its primary purpose.

> Jose,
>
> I'd like to suggest that you prepare and distribute an agenda several days before each monthly meeting.
>
> I realized last time that people are wasting time coming to meetings they really don't have to attend because they don't have an agenda ahead of time. Also, people come unprepared to discuss issues because they don't know in advance what we'll cover.
>
> I'll be glad to help in any way I can; just let me know.

I THINK THE PURPOSE IS TO ...

EXERCISE 1.4

Think of the document you're planning for your own job, and identify your purpose here.

Step 3. Identify your main point

After you identify your primary purpose, identify the most important point — whatever you want your reader to do or to know. Imagine you only had five or ten seconds to get your point across — say, that an elevator door was closing or a car was driving away:

- Your most important point is what you'd shout out to seize that window of time
- You could also call this your message's key sentence, topic sentence, or takeaway

Don't worry if your main point sounds abrupt or doesn't immediately unpack all the details the reader will need to know at the end. You'll be able to add more information in Step 4.

Here's an example with the email you saw on p. 8. Depending on the interests of Eileen's reader and on Eileen's purpose for writing, her main point could go in either of two directions:

> TO INFORM ONLY: Three-shift coverage works well.
>
> TO PERSUADE: Please let me know what you decide about our ongoing coverage.

Many full business messages are very short — e.g., a text message, or a quick project update in a cloud-based collaboration tool. In these cases, writing out your main point can mean you've successfully completed your entire message.

Chapter 2 includes strategies to highlight your main point in any kind of multiparagraph document, and Chapter 4 includes strategies to choose the right words for any statement. For now, remember that clear writing requires you to identify exactly who your audience is and to identify what your purpose and most important message are.

EXERCISE 1.5

Which of the emails below has a clear main point? (Check Appendix A for the answer.)

Email A

Dear Mr. Weller:

Safety is our number-one concern, and our safety record shows that we are all trained well. There is a lot of traffic on the block of Jefferson Street between South Main and Mission. The street often sees heavy traffic, yet its current condition is a safety hazard. The street should probably be widened. That would have significant benefits, and we could certainly get the job done. A night permit would allow us to start right away.

Email B

Dear Mr. Weller:

I am writing to ask you to give my construction company a noise permit to allow night work on the block of Jefferson Street between South Main and Mission. The street often sees heavy traffic, yet its current condition is a safety hazard.

Widening the street would have significant benefits, and we are ready to work day and night to make the necessary repairs.

We hope to begin work as soon as possible. If you have any questions, please call me at my office.

•

Writers can neglect to include a clear main point for two main reasons:

- They're thinking out loud more than they're sending a consciously formulated idea
- Or they have a main point but hesitate to state it directly

But business readers are busy people: they don't have time to guess about your meaning. It's your task as a professional person to express your most important message clearly. So whenever you're asking for a reader's time, take the time to compose a main point that's clear and complete.

One clear, possible message can be "I think the following considerations are important, but I haven't reached a conclusion yet." Always try to make that fact clear, if that's why you're including some details in an email or memo. Also try to apply Steps 4 and 5 below to answer your readers' questions and to clarify your logic.

Step 4. Answer your readers' questions

It's often necessary to help readers grasp information or grasp the benefit of taking action. Some good judgment can be necessary to decide how much contextual detail your readers will need to see.

You may face a balancing act:

- You don't want to make readers circle back to you with questions that you didn't answer
- But you don't want to waste their time with unnecessary information either

Here's a three-step method to answer all the readers' questions and to organize your information logically.

1. Read your most important message aloud, and brainstorm a full list of questions that your readers might have. Aim to have, say, five to seven questions if your message is longer than two pages.

2. Answer each question, and organize the answers in a logical way, e.g., through one of these organizational tactics:
   - With a timeline
   - By comparing pros and cons
   - By listing how results have either met or not met your criteria
   - In ascending or descending order, cost, priority, etc.

3. Delete any details that don't seem essential, and make sure you haven't repeated any details.

EXERCISE 1.6

Think of the document you're planning for your own job. Write out your main point here.

Now list at least five questions that readers could have about your statement, and then answer each question.

- **READER QUESTION AND ANSWER:**

- **READER QUESTION AND ANSWER:**

- **READER QUESTION AND ANSWER:**

- **READER QUESTION AND ANSWER:**

- **READER QUESTION AND ANSWER:**

Step 5. Organize your information

Organizing information is a subjective process: two coworkers might organize the same information in two completely different ways that are equally effective. Common organization tactics include setting out pros and cons, contrasting advantages and disadvantages, and listing completed steps versus steps that remain.

EXERCISE 1.7

These two groups have three items each. For each group, name a quality that the three items have in common.

GROUP A	GROUP B
hammers	paper clips
nails	staples
paint	white-out

The items in Group A are supplies you could get in a hardware store, while the items in Group B are office supplies. Are there any other logical ways you could reorganize these items under a different grouping?

Here's one attempt.

GROUP A	GROUP B
paint	hammers
white-out	nails
	paper clips
	staples

Now the items in Group A are things you wouldn't want to spill, while the items in Group B are solid tools. To stay clear, you'd want to explain that organizational strategy if you sent someone these two groupings of items.

There is no single right or wrong way to organize information, as long as it's organized by come clearly recognizable logic that prevents readers from having to put in their own guesswork. It doesn't usually insult readers' intelligence when you explain your thinking. Explanations can prevent unnecessary guesswork and keep your logic easy to follow.

EXERCISE 1.8

Suppose you're writing a newsletter article about athletic activities that your company might sponsor. Here's one way you might organize them:

WATER-RELATED		NOT WATER-RELATED	
surfing	water skiing	basketball	rollerblading
canoeing	scuba diving	rock climbing	mountain biking
wind surfing	kayaking	football	tennis
swimming		jogging	volleyball
		snowboarding	baseball
		mountain climbing	

Now you try it. Organize the activities another way:

- surfing
- water skiing
- wind surfing
- snowboarding
- mountain biking
- rollerblading
- swimming
- scuba diving
- football
- basketball
- canoeing
- tennis
- volleyball
- baseball
- mountain climbing
- rock climbing
- kayaking
- jogging

EXERCISE 1.9

Think of the document you're planning for your own job. In Exercise 1.6, you answered the questions your readers are most likely to have.

Now organize those answers in a logical way, for instance, by applying one of the organizational tactics listed in Step 2 of the three-step system on p. 12.

EXERCISE 1.10

Review your audience analysis, purpose for writing, main point, readers' questions, and organizational scheme. These five completed steps add up to your writing plan.

Apply your plan now by writing out a quick first draft of your document here or on some scratch paper (some is included on pp. 58–59).

2   WRITE TO GET RESULTS

This chapter shows you how to format a longer message to advance your purpose and get the results you need by sizing up a longer document. When you're done, you'll be ready to use different document sections to help readers follow your ideas, grasp what's important, and grasp what comes next in your exchange of messages.

Different people may solve the same writing challenge differently, but some best practices still apply. For instance, readers always grasp your information or request more easily when you state your main point right away, in the subject line or opening paragraph.

The journalistic triangle

Have you ever noticed that the first paragraphs of many news articles contain the most important information? The rest of the article then provides further details that support, explain, expand on, or illustrate that information.

News editors know that readers often scan only the headline and first part of an article. They also know that the final paragraphs of a piece may drop out or go onto separate webpages. That's why editors often answer readers' most important question right at the beginning, as shown in the business example below.

Putting the most important information first helps you answer the readers' most important question right away. It also helps you establish context for the details that follow.

Sales in the third quarter were nearly five percent above the company's set goals.

Answer to the most important question

•

Quarterly sales figures

Details

•

Goals for the fourth quarter

Further details

Subject lines

A subject line is the most valuable real estate in any message that has one, so be careful not to squander it. A subject line is often a perfect place to spell out your main point.

ARE YOU WRITING TO INFORM? Spell out your central topic, e.g.,

- **SUBJECT:** XYZ report details
- **SUBJECT:** Agenda for XYZ meeting
- **SUBJECT:** Contact info for XYZ stakeholders

ARE YOU WRITING TO PERSUADE? Spell out the action in question, e.g.,

- **SUBJECT:** Please send XYZ report
- **SUBJECT:** Can you speak on Topics X, Y, & Z on Tues.?
- **SUBJECT:** Need contact info for XYZ

Each of these subject lines signals the writer's primary purpose. Readers who clicked on emails under those subject lines should see well-organized details to expand on the central informative topic or the central persuasive point.

It would also be easy to recast any of these lines as opening sentences for a text, note, or business letter that didn't have a subject line:

	SUBJECT LINE WITH A SIMPLE IDEA	**THE SAME IDEA IN A SENTENCE OR TWO**
TO INFORM	XYZ report details	Here are the details you requested for the XYZ report.
	Agenda for XYZ meeting	Here's the agenda for the XYZ meeting on Tuesday at 2 in our main conference room.
TO PERSUADE	Please send XYZ report	I need the XYZ report. Can you send it by 2pm?
	Can you speak on Topics X, Y, & Z on Tues.?	Can you speak on Topics X, Y, and Z at the meeting on Tues.?

Here are some further tips to keep subject lines easy to follow and act on.

Stay specific and descriptive

A subject line can be your first and most important opportunity to get your message across — or to get your email opened in the first place. Notice how the original and revised subject lines expand in the following examples:

VAGUE: Changes

SPECIFIC: Health benefits will change on Dec. 1: Please enroll

VAGUE: Planning date

SPECIFIC: Planning project: Is meeting on Apr. 2, 6, or 9?

Be clear, concise, and honest

A compelling subject line gets the message across without inaccurate claims, unnecessary words, or cryptic abbreviations.

WORDY AND CONFUSING: This msg inclds new details abt our accessories

CONCISE AND CLEAR: Introducing free returns on accessories

It's best for a subject line to stay as concise as possible, but not at the expense of clarity. Chapter 3 includes tips on both concise language and clear language.

Include a call to action

It's also a good idea to use the subject line to signal any actions you'll request in the body of your message. Notice how the original and revised subject lines expand in the following examples:

VAGUE: New article

SPECIFIC: Please read "The Scary Consequences of Poor Time Management"

VAGUE: Time cards

SPECIFIC: Need to get paid? Submit time cards by 1pm Fri.

EXERCISE 2.1

Think of the message you're planning for your own job. If the document does have a subject line, write one out and try to make it specific, descriptive, clear, and concise.

If your message doesn't have a subject line, you'll be able to follow these same guidelines later on for your opening paragraph.

A CHECKLIST TO HELP ANY EMAIL GET RESULTS

☐ Have you crafted your subject line carefully? It may help readers decide whether to open the email in the first place.

☐ Have you paid attention to the To and CC lines?

- People on the To line should recognize that they may need to respond to the email.
- The CC line signals that people on it should *not* need to respond, and they can probably read the message at their leisure.

☐ Have you made sure your language is specific? Chapter 3 includes some sentence-level tips, and here are two especially important considerations:

- Do you need a response?
  - If so, spell out the time you hope to hear back from your readers.
  - If not, consider saying so. It takes some pressure off, and it makes it more clear that you're writing to inform.
- Do you need someone to stick to a deadline? If so, spell it out in the opening paragraph.

☐ Have you proofread the text, including the subject line? (Chapter 4 includes some tips on how.)

UPDATING AN EMAIL THREAD'S SUBJECT LINE

Another good email strategy is to change the subject line to reflect a shift in topic or to highlight a new request. Changing the subject line can also make it much easier to locate a buried, important detail weeks later without having to look at dozens of identical subject lines.

Opening paragraphs

If a document doesn't have a subject line, it's even more important for the opening paragraph to be specific. After your opening paragraph, readers should not be in any suspense about why they're spending their time on your message.

For documents longer than a paragraph, make sure your opening spells out your primary purpose in writing. Your opening can also establish a personal connection.

Subject lines can have a wide range of grammatical structures, while the opening paragraph is your chance to deliver your main point in complete, professional sentences. (See Chapter 4 for a few grammar tips.)

EXERCISE 2.2

For your own message, imagine that your readers might only look through your opening paragraph and then move on to another task. Can you use the paragraph to deliver the message they'll absolutely need?

Try it by writing the opening paragraph for your document here.

Conclusions

For documents longer than several paragraphs, consider repeating your main point at the end. Maybe you've included a lot of supplementary information in a message that also includes a request. In that case, readers may need a quick reminder at the end.

Your conclusion can also re-establish a personal connection, as the note you'll end on.

EXERCISE 2.3

Write the conclusion for your document here.

KEEPING SENTENCES AND PARAGRAPHS EASY TO READ

Try to keep your sentences under 30 words or so: anything longer demands too much concentration and slows a busy reader down. Also, try to mix longer and shorter sentences together to add variety to your text.

Paragraphs also become more difficult to read the longer they are, but there's no set-in-concrete rule for paragraph length. About 120 words can be a good limit. Try to recognize that length in your writing, then start feeling concerned, step back, and look for a good point to start a new paragraph to cleanly separate your ideas.

Salutations and greetings

Salutations help establish a cordial tone in letters and emails. They encourage people to listen to an informative message or to feel willing to take action for a persuasive request. Salutations also assure readers that the message is meant for them.

A personalized approach is powerful: you're more likely to get someone's attention when you call them by name (e.g., "Hi Sue") or use the name for a team they're associated with ("Dear Accounting team").

It only takes a few seconds to include a salutation and the person's name, and the benefits are huge. So we suggest including salutations for each first message you write and only drop the salutation if the message chain continues.

Here are some sample salutations for people outside your organization, or higher up in it:

- "Dear Mr. / Ms. / Dr. X" is usually safe for formal letters and emails to senior clients, customers, or coworkers.
- "Dear X" is more formal than "Hello," which is more formal than "Hi."

Closings

Closings also affect your tone. It only takes a few seconds to include a closing and your name, and the benefits are huge. You're usually safe with "Regards" or "Best."

You can also use "Thank you" as a closing or as a standalone statement. Closings tend to be more effective when they refer to something specific:

> Thank you for hosting the event last week.
>
> Best regards,
>
> Deedee

Think carefully about the effects any religious closings or any intended humor may have in your professional context.

Attachments

For an email a few paragraphs long, use your opening paragraph to mention any attachments. Don't assume that readers will simply notice an attachment or open it. Instead, send a clear heads-up that the file is there, and summarize the important points so readers will have a compelling reason to open it.

- If your purpose is to inform, spell out the topic in the subject or opening paragraph.

- If you need readers to do something with a file, then add a note to the subject line, opening paragraph, or both. (E.g., "Please edit attached doc," or "If you have any questions about this file, I'll need you to send them to me by 9am. Please also be ready to summarize the file's details at the 10 o'clock meeting.")

If the message is more than a few paragraphs, consider repeating the request in your conclusion. (E.g., "Thanks for editing this ASAP" or "Tomorrow by 9 I'll look for any questions you have.")

EXERCISE 2.4

If you're sending an attachment, answer these questions for your own document.

- What happens if readers don't open the attachment?
- How will you make sure they notice the file and know what to do with it?

Lists

You can use a list in business writing whenever you present three or more related pieces of information. In fact, lists are usually the best way to present a series of two or more items because lists do three things:

- Communicate information quickly
- Save writing time
- Reduce the chance of grammar and punctuation errors

These five guidelines keep any list easy to read. Full illustrations of each guideline are below.

A. Set the format
B. Introduce the list
C. Make sure all items belong
D. Maintain parallel form
E. Organize and limit the items

A. Set the format

For a bulleted list, you should be able to rearrange the items in any order without changing the meaning. In contrast, a numbered list should be in chronological order or should follow a ranking system (e.g., first prize, second prize, etc.).

Here are two more considerations:

- A lettered list (A., B., C., D., E.) doesn't imply as strong a chronological order as numbers do. We've used a lettered list above for these five list guidelines since you could follow the guidelines in a different order with the same result.
- Letters or numbers both make it easy to refer to "Step 4 above" or "Item H on p. 4" when you need readers to go back and locate a previous item in a list.

Most people don't stop to think about these kinds of list formatting, but they can make a huge difference in clarity.

List formatting is an example of how writing demands more energy and care than reading does. The extra effort of carefully formatting a list can earn your readers' respect and showcase your talent as an analytical thinker. Namely, it can show that you've clearly identified an overarching theme and assembled smaller details that illustrate that theme.

B. Introduce the list

No list in an email or letter should stand alone: a list always needs an introductory statement if it's set in the middle of paragraphs of text. (A list in a presentation slide is an exception when the list items fall under a clear slide heading.)

Also note that the first item in a list can't introduce the list itself.

INCORRECT, WITHOUT AN INTRODUCTION:

- We offer several thank-you gifts
- A 10% discount on purchases during May
- A discount coupon for the Milano Ristorante
- A complimentary bottle of our best olive oil

CORRECT, WITH AN INTRODUCTION:

In appreciation for your business, we offer three thank-you gifts:

- A 10% discount on purchases during May
- A discount coupon for the Milano Ristorante
- A complimentary bottle of our best olive oil

C. Make sure all items belong

Make sure all items belong in a list: they should all relate directly to the unifying theme in the list's introductory statement.

NOT ALL ITEMS RELATE TO THE INTRODUCTORY STATEMENT:

To prepare the room for training, please do the following:

- Set up the tables in a U shape
- Put two flipcharts in the front of the classroom
- Place the projector on the table in the corner
- Make sure participants will have lots of exercises and opportunities to practice

(REVISED ON THE NEXT PAGE)

To prepare <u>yourself</u> to deliver the training, <u>add lots of participant exercises and opportunities to practice</u>. To prepare <u>the training room</u>, please do the following:

- Set up the tables in a U shape
- Put two flipcharts in the front of the classroom
- Place the projector on the table in the corner

D. Maintain parallel form

Keep all list items parallel by presenting them in the same grammatical forms. For example, if one item begins with a past-tense verb, start all the list items with past-tense verbs.

Also be consistent with initial capitalization (e.g., having all items start in lowercase, or having all items start with a capital letter) and be consistent with sentence structure (e.g., having all items be sentence fragments, or having all items be complete sentences).

NOT PARALLEL:

The agenda for the March meeting includes the following:

- <u>Discussion</u> of the new health plan, which will be available to all permanent full-time employ<u>ees</u>
- <u>Whether</u> to revise the procedures manu<u>al</u>
- <u>Draft</u> an early-retirement polic<u>y.</u>

PARALLEL:

At the March meeting, we will do the following:

- <u>Discuss</u> the new health plan, which will be available to all permanent full-time employ<u>ees</u>
- <u>Decide</u> whether to revise the procedures manu<u>al</u>
- <u>Draft</u> an early-retirement poli<u>cy</u>

E. Organize and limit the items

As a general rule, keep lists under six items or so. When long lists are necessary, try to reorganize them as two or more shorter lists with main points and one or more levels of subpoints.

TOO MANY ITEMS:

Please supply the following for the conference that begins on October 22:

- 30 printed workbooks for each meeting room
- 30 handouts
- An overhead projector for each meeting room
- Coffee, tea, and pastry in the foyer each morning
- Four round tables for each meeting room
- A basket of fruit for each table in the meeting rooms
- A registration table in the foyer

ITEMS ORGANIZED WITH SUBPOINTS IN TWO LEVELS:

Please supply the following items for the conference that begins on October 22:

- In each meeting room:
  - 30 each of the following:
    - printed workbooks
    - handouts
  - An overhead projector
  - Four round tables
  - A basket of fruit for each table
- In the foyer:
  - Coffee, tea, and pastry each morning
  - A registration table

Remember that if a long list is unavoidable, you can use letters rather than numbers (**A., B., C., D., E.**). Lettered and numbered lists make it easy to refer to specific points such as "Item H" or "Item 12" if you need to single out just one item from among many list items.

EXERCISE 2.5

Use the space below or a blank sheet of paper to rewrite this paragraph in list format. (Check Appendix A for one possible answer.)

> The task force found that the customer service representatives need training in how to respond to problems and complaints. There is widespread unhappiness about the quality of food in the cafeteria, indicating the need to find another vendor. How to implement flexible hours without creating logistical problems requires additional study. Finally, field representatives need newer tablets, which have not been included in this year's budget. These are the primary areas of concern the members of the task force believe they need to address during the next six months.

EXERCISE 2.6

Use the space below or a blank sheet of paper to rewrite and reformat this paragraph as a list.

> To help us update our database, please review the enclosed listings and notify us of any changes. First, proofread each listing and indicate any necessary corrections. Then please enter the best address for clients to reach you, and at the same time verify that the telephone numbers and email addresses are correct. Finally, if you wish, you may add a maximum of two lines of explanation to each listing.

3   USE CONCISE, CLEAR LANGUAGE

> I didn't have time to write a short letter, so I wrote a long one instead.
>
> — MARK TWAIN

Would you rather read a three-page memo, or a single-page memo that includes all the same facts? Concise writing takes some effort, but readers appreciate it, and the skills are easy to add to your toolkit.

Some writers try to impress their readers with complicated language, while other writers send complicated messages because they're careless or in a hurry. Both approaches can result in confusion, irritation, and lost respect.

The most effective and impressive writing makes complex ideas seem simple and clear — an achievement that usually takes time for the writer. Complicated, long-winded language slows your readers down and can make your message boring. Clear, concise writing holds readers' interest and helps you get the results you need.

Concise language

Three strategies are especially helpful to keep language focused:

- Use one word for a one-word idea
- Avoid repetition
- Keep language active

Use one word for a one-word idea

Sometimes you can collapse several words or a long phrase into a single word that conveys your message quickly and clearly. For instance, *at a time prior to* simply means *before*. The single word is more effective.

At other times, you can collapse a multiword phrase into one word in three steps:

1. Identify the most important word or idea
2. Turn it into a different part of speech
3. Cut out words that don't enhance your meaning

- **ORIGINAL:** We <u>are in agreement</u> with you about the contract terms.
- **REVISION:** We <u>agree</u> with you about the contract terms.

- **ORIGINAL:** She solved the problem <u>in a short amount of time</u>.
- **REVISION:** She solved the problem <u>quickly</u>.

EXERCISE 3.1

Eliminate unnecessary words in these sentences. (Check Appendix A for the answers.)

- **ORIGINAL:** The client visited the <u>site of the project</u> in May.
- **REVISION:** The client visited the <u>project site</u> in May.

1. We conducted a survey of the members.

2. Our manager made an offer to buy everyone coffee.

3. I believe this procedure will make an improvement in the way we file reports.

4. He called us in regard to his recent insurance claim.

Avoid repetition

Here are some repetitive phrases that make sentences unnecessarily long:

- alternative choices
- basic fundamentals
- serious crisis
- final outcome
- past experience
- surrounding circumstances
- equally as effective as
- symptoms indicative of
- desirable benefits
- important essentials
- end result
- future plans
- separate entities
- advance warning
- two halves
- regular weekly meetings
- absolutely complete
- 10am in the morning

A crisis is always serious, plans are always for the future, and 10am never happens at night. Cutting repetitive words will save your readers time.

EXERCISE 3.2

Eliminate the unnecessary repetitions in these sentences.

1. The urban residents of the city are unhappy with the new regulations.

2. The subterranean garage, located underground, is more secure than the old one.

3. Until last week, our group had the best record to date.

Keep language active

Passive language can weaken your writing, confuse your readers, and make your sentences longer. In contrast, active language focuses your readers' attention and increases the impact of your ideas.

For active language, say who acts and not just what the action is. The actor comes before the action in the following revisions.

PASSIVE: The team's document **has been completed**.

ACTIVE: The team **has completed** the document.

PASSIVE: A safety plan **was prepared and distributed** to employees by the committee.

ACTIVE: The committee **prepared** a safety plan **and distributed** it to employees.

It can be frustrating and confusing to try to follow instructions in passive language. In the following case, the implied actor is you — the reader.

> **Passive:** The cover of the printer **should be lifted,** the ink cartridges that **have been emptied should be removed,** and the new ink cartridges **should be opened, prepared, and inserted** in the appropriate slots.

> **Active:** **Lift** the printer cover, **remove** the empty cartridges, **open and prepare** the
> *[implied* you*]* new cartridges, **and insert** them into the appropriate slot.

EXERCISE 3.3

Revise these sentences to be active, direct, and clear. The first step is to identify an actor; feel free to invent one.

1. The research project is being conducted by the News Department.

2. A copy of the approval must be stapled to the request before it is forwarded to the Accounting Office.

3. The new design is attached for your review and its return by March 15 would be appreciated.

Clear language

Two strategies are especially helpful to keep language clear:

- Stay specific
- Use plain English

Stay specific

The more specific your language is, the less guesswork and effort your readers will need to understand you.

> **VAGUE:** Our group went to Los Angeles for a meeting. I'll send you the meeting minutes so you can understand our next steps.

> **SPECIFIC:** Our project team <u>flew</u> to Los Angeles <u>to meet with Harriet Allen, the system designer.</u> I'll send you the meeting minutes so you can understand our next steps.

> **VAGUE:** Ask the client to complete the paperwork in a timely manner.

> **SPECIFIC:** Ask the client to complete <u>the new account application form within 10 working days.</u>

Vague language can require readers to guess at unknown meanings behind your word choices, so it can show consideration to supply precise information instead. The following word choices start out vague and then grow more specific:

VAGUE:	SPECIFIC:
vehicle	car
car	self-driving car
traveled	flew; took the train; sailed
contacted	called; spoke to; visited
some	five
recently	yesterday
in a timely manner	by August 15th; within two weeks

EXERCISE 3.4

Underline the vague, general words and phrases in these sentences. Then use your imagination to fill in details and revise the sentences so they communicate specific, useful information.

1. Recently, we looked at a structure that might be suitable for our needs.

2. We have identified a few items to be discussed at the meeting, so please leave considerable time in your schedule.

Use plain English

Plain English communicates your message more reliably than overly formal words and phrases. Too much formality can waste time by forcing readers to mentally translate your writing into everyday language.

How long does it take for you to read this paragraph and understand it?

> Per your request, enclosed herewith are documents concerning the above-mentioned project. Please review said documents and return them to this office prior to January 15th. We will then initiate the process of implementing the requested system modifications.

See how much easier the paragraph is to read when it's written in plain English?

> As you asked, I am sending a description of the XYZ project. Please read it and send it back to me before January 15th, and then we will start the system modifications.

KEEPING CHARTS CLEAR

Charts can make numeric data much more clear than sentences can. Chart types include pie charts for percentages, line charts to show a trend in data, and bar charts for data in groups.

Whatever form is the best fit for your numeric data, keep your chart design simple. If you're concerned that a chart may deepen the complexity of your message without enhancing its clarity, then either look for ways to simplify the chart or consider leaving it out.

Refer to the chart and its location as soon as the reader might need to turn to it, e.g., "See p. 8 for these percentages." Also try to place the chart close to any text it helps explain.

EXERCISE 3.5

Here's one last exercise on clear language. Some of the words in this list can be good, precise word choices. But writers often use these formal-sounding words when simpler language would communicate more clearly.

What ordinary words or phrases would be good alternatives to these words? Use a thesaurus or dictionary if you're not sure.

1. prior to

2. subsequent to

3. utilize

4. supplemental

5. heretofore

6. commence

7. endeavor

4   PRESENT A PROFESSIONAL IMAGE

This final chapter focuses on two strategies to sound professional and also prevent your language from distracting readers:

- Nonstandard grammar and punctuation can disrupt readers' concentration and send incorrect signals about how ideas connect. The first chapter section includes strategies for **KEEPING LANGUAGE CORRECT** and crisp.

- While typos can creep into any document, **PROOFREADING** also helps make sure that readers stay focused on your ideas alone — not the writing mechanics.

Grammar, punctuation, and word choice

Many business writers would project a more professional image if they brushed up on their grammar and word knowledge. Here are four refresher areas:

- Commonly misused words
- Apostrophes
- Commas
- Colons and semicolons

Commonly misused words

Here are seven sets of words that many business writers confuse.

CITE / SIGHT / SITE

The attorney **cited** similar cases.

VERB: to quote or to refer to

She traveled on, loving each new **sight.**

NOUN: something a person could see

The new warehouse will be built on the **site.**

NOUN: physical location; collection of webpages

NOTE: *Cite* is the root of *citation*. *Sight* is spelled like *light*, and both words relate to vision.

ITS / IT'S

I think **it's** a good idea.

CONTRACTION: "it is" or "it has"

The advertising agency lost **its** biggest client.

Possessive form of *it*

NOTE: If you're not sure whether to use the apostrophe, try substituting "it is" or "it has." If either works, use *it's*.

LEAD / LED

Place a **lead** apron on the patient's lap for X-rays.

NOUN: a metal (rhymes with *bed*)

The facilitator **led** the discussion.

Past tense of the verb *to lead* (rhymes with *bed*)

Do they **lead** the discussions?

Present or future tense of the verb *to lead* (rhymes with *seed*)

THAN / THEN

Isaac accepted congratulations for his sales record and **then** thanked his associates.

At that time

Anik can complete her statistical assessments faster **than** anyone else in the department.

The word sets up a comparison

NOTE: *Then* is spelled like *when*, and both words refer to time.

THERE / THEIR / THEY'RE

There was an accident.

A word to indicate an event or place

Their car was badly damaged.

Possessive form of *them*

They're moving to a new house.

CONTRACTION: "they are"

NOTE: *There* contains the word *here*, and both words can refer to place.

TO / TOO / TWO

Let me know if I should go **to** the meeting.

A preposition meaning *toward*

I want **to** go out.

First word of an infinitive verb

Danny takes on **too** many tasks.

Excessively

Two desserts are included.

The spelled-out number *2*

NOTE: Spell out any number (e.g., "Two" or "Fifty-three") at the start of a sentence.

YOUR / YOU'RE

Your proposal has been approved.

A possessive word

You're being transferred to another department.

CONTRACTION: "you are"

NOTE: *Your* contains the word *our*, and both words show possession.

EXERCISE 4.1

Write in the correct word from the list below for the blank in each sentence. More than one word may be appropriate. (Check Appendix A for the answers.)

there	their	they're	your	you're
its	it's	to	too	two

1. The sale doesn't start until next week, and _____ not possible for us to offer you the special price until then.

2. _____ many trees are being uprooted for the new development and not being replanted.

3. _____ seems to have been some confusion about the agenda for Friday's meeting.

4. Our department almost lost _____ certification during last week's evaluation.

5. Please let me know whether _____ going to attend Barney's retirement party.

Apostrophes

Apostrophes take different positions to show possession. When the word is singular, you usually show possession by adding an apostrophe + -s, whether or not the word ends in an s sound:

the monitor's screen	Chris's question	anyone's guess
my driver's van	somebody's coat	

Most plural words end in or -s or -es. To form their possessive, place the apostrophe after the final s:

the students' progress	two weeks' worth of work
the buses' tires	others' contributions

Some plural nouns don't end in -s; in that case, you indicate possession by adding an apostrophe + -s:

the mice's mouse pads	the children's toys
the two women's offices	

The only time you add an apostrophe to create a plural is for lowercase letters of the alphabet. (Acronyms don't need apostrophes since they're uppercase, and plural numbers don't need apostrophes.) All the following plural forms are correct:

CORRECT <u>WITH</u> AN APOSTROPHE:

Where are the *x's* and *y's*?

CORRECT <u>WITHOUT</u> AN APOSTROPHE:

* Most of our custome<u>rs</u> are in their <u>30s</u>.
* Our firm was founded in the 19<u>70s</u>.
* There are two ban<u>ks</u> with AT<u>Ms</u> on this block.
* I'll walk you through the d<u>os</u> and don'<u>ts</u>.

EXERCISE 4.2

Add apostrophes to words in these four phrases to make them possessive:

EXAMPLE:

one carpenters hammer → one carpenter's hammer

1. the directors office
2. several days backlog
3. the mens desks
4. anyones wallet

Now form the plural for these two items:

5. RFP
6. 1980

Commas

Here are four rules for using commas.

A. COMMAS AND COMPLETE SENTENCES

The most common type of run-on sentence uses nothing but a comma to join two word groups that could stand on their own as complete sentences.

INCORRECT, RUN-ON SENTENCE:

The researchers collected all the data on time, they did not make their findings public for six months.

This mistake is also called a *comma splice*; they're increasingly common in social media writing, but they can make business writers look overly casual or uninformed. Here are the two word groups that could stand on their own as complete sentences:

• The researchers collected all the data on time

• They did not make their findings public for six months

Here are three ways to correct that run-on sentence:

1. Break the sentence in two, add a period, and capitalize the start of the second sentence:

> The researchers collected all the data on time. They did not make their findings public for six months.

2. Follow the comma with a conjunction:

> The researchers collected all the data on time, but they did not make their findings public for six months.

3. Or change the structure of the sentence by adding words and punctuation that signal how the two facts relate to each other:

> While the researchers collected all the data on time, they did not make their findings public for six months.

> The researchers collected all the data on time; however, they did not make their findings public for six months.

B. COMMAS FOR ITEMS IN A SERIES

Many people wonder whether to use a comma before "and" in a series or three or more items (sometimes called the *serial comma*). It is always necessary to use the serial comma if the sentence might be confusing without it.

In the following example, it's hard to tell which tasks go together. A serial comma before the final "and" clears up the confusion.

CONFUSING: The activities included seminars on marketing, workshops on newsletter design and promotion and preparation for a sales campaign.

CLEAR: The activities included seminars on marketing, workshops on newsletter design, and promotion and preparation for a sales campaign.

But it's usually fine to either use the serial comma *or* leave it out when your sentences list a few simple items that it's easy to tell apart. Just try to be consistent with that decision across all your sentences.

One easy choice is to always use the serial comma. Then you'll never have to stop and ask yourself if the last comma is necessary to keep a particular sentence clear.

C. COMMAS AND CONJUNCTIONS

Be careful not to put a comma after a conjunction, rather than before it.

INCORRECT: I've read a lot of proposals <u>but, I've</u> never written one.

CORRECT: I've read a lot of <u>proposals, but</u> I've never written one.

D. COMMAS AFTER AN INTRODUCTORY IDEA

Many sentences begin with a word group that introduces the main point. These introductory words usually tell the reader something about the main action of the sentence — such as establishing when, where, how, why, or the surrounding conditions.

A comma signals the end of an introductory word group and indicates that the main part of the sentence is about to begin. This kind of comma prevents confusion by keeping the introductory words from running into the main part of the sentence.

CONFUSING: If Sue asks Joe will deliver the proposals.

CLEAR: If Sue <u>asks, Joe</u> will deliver the proposals.

Colons and semicolons

A semicolon separates thoughts more decisively than a comma does, but less decisively than a period does. There are three main situations when you use a semicolon:

A. To join two complete-sentence word groups with two loosely related ideas:

   Amanda called in <u>sick;</u> I wonder if she has the flu.

B. With a comma, to set off certain transitional words:

   Amanda has the <u>flu; therefore,</u> she called in sick.

C. To separate items in a series when one or more items contain internal commas:

   The representatives are Bob Dorfman, <u>treasurer;</u> Sandra Scarlesi, vice <u>president;</u> and Thomas Jackson, secretary.

In contrast, a colon means "Here's the explanation," "Here's the list," or "Here's what the person said." Here are some examples:

> Sam is concerned about the presentation: he thinks it's too long and unfocused.

> Please send me the following items: your budget requests, last month's expense reports, and projections of expected income.

> We found some problems: poor soil conditions, loose gravel, tree stumps that need to be removed, and an underground stream.

Traditionally, you only use a colon after a word group that could stand on its own as a complete sentence. I.e., you only add a colon if you could correctly add a period instead and create a new sentence, as in "We found some problems. Namely, we found poor soil ...."

This rule is fading out when a word group introduces a bulleted or numbered list. But the traditional rule can still make your writing look polished when you use a full sentence and final colon to head any given list.

UNTRADITIONAL:

Please supply:

- 30 printed workbooks for each meeting room
- 30 handouts

TRADITIONAL AND POLISHED:

Please supply the following:

- 30 printed workbooks for each meeting room
- 30 handouts

The first option wouldn't work as a complete sentence, as in "Please supply." But you could make a complete sentence out of "Please supply the following."

It's still nonstandard to use a colon *inside* a sentence after word groups such as "We carry water bottles in: blue, green, and orange" or "I'm going to: catch up with email, meet with a client, and finish the paperwork." Those two series of sentence items simply don't need a colon before them.

The colons would only be standard if the underlined word groups could form complete sentences in themselves, such as "Here are the three colors: X, Y, and Z" and "I'm going to do the following: X, Y, and Z." (I.e., you could replace each of those colons with a period and then have a complete new sentence instead.)

EXERCISE 4.3

Think about the semicolon or colon in each of these sentences, and write in the correct punctuation.

1. Your order should arrive by May 12th at the latest; our records indicate that it was shipped to your Denver office on May 4th.

2. I'll start managing the XYZ project next month: I'm sure we'll need your help.

3. The consultant recommended that we put all of our procedure manuals online: she billed for three days of work last week.

4. I am ready to: interview five applicants, decide who is most qualified, and hire two people.

Proofreading and tone

Here are five tips to prevent readers from being distracted by typos:

- **Take breaks between writing the first draft and proofreading it** to give yourself a fresher eye for what you've written.

- **Zoom in so the text is large** — making errors easier to see. Or try proofreading from a printed page after you've written on a screen so the text looks different.

- **Try reading your work out loud,** asking yourself if the sentences sound correct when you hear them.

- **Run your spell-checker slowly,** being especially careful with distinctive product, organization, and individual names.

- **Make sure you haven't misspelled any information in the date, address blocks, or subject line.** And don't forget to proof headings. They're especially easy to overlook because they act as signposts to point you forward to the text that follows them.

And finally, check the tone of your message before you send it. Do the written words match the mood you'd want to convey if you could use your voice?

Abrupt:	Get me the revisions by Thursday.
Polite:	Please be sure to get me the revisions by Thursday.
Hurried:	Got a lot on my plate right now — not sure I can take on a new gig.
Professional:	I'm very busy this month, and I'm not able to take on a new project.
Stuffy:	Prior to July 23rd, payments can be sent only through the Postal Service. Subsequent to that date, payments must be made through our website.
Polite:	Before July 23rd, we can accept payments by mail only. After July 23rd, we can accept payments only through our website.

COACHING COWORKERS ON THEIR WRITING

Coaching coworkers on their writing skills requires tact, and you should check with your manager about whether it's OK for you to offer any writing tips on your own. If coaching does seem right and helpful, here are four considerations to keep in mind.

A. **TRY TO STAY IMPERSONAL,** e.g.,

- "<u>You're</u> using insider jargon in customer emails" could sound pointed.

- But it takes some of the heat off when you focus on *readers'* needs instead: "<u>Customers</u> might be confused by this insider term we use here in the office."

B. *I* **STATEMENTS ARE MORE TACTFUL IF THE CONTEXT REALLY IS PERSONAL,** e.g.,

- It could sound pointed to say, "<u>You shouldn't</u> email me full news articles with no explanations when I'm on the road. Just send me the upshot instead."

- It's more tactful to use an *I* statement to explain, "When <u>I'm</u> mobile, <u>I never have time</u> to read a full news article. Would you send me quick summaries of just the relevant parts?"

C. **FOCUS ON THE BENEFITS OF CAREFUL WRITING AND NOT THE DRAW-BACKS OF PROBLEMATIC WRITING,** e.g.,

- "<u>Nobody wants</u> to read paragraphs that are a page long" could sound pointed, even if it's true.

- Instead, it's both true and positive to say, "Shorter paragraphs and lists are <u>easier to skim</u> because they break up the topics."

D. **FINALLY, A BOOK OF GENERAL ADVICE ON WRITING SKILLS CAN SEEM LESS POINTED THAN A NOTE OR A FACE-TO-FACE REQUEST.** See Appendix B for a list of topics we cover in our own books on business communication skills. The book topics range from essential grammar to emails, proposals, presentations, and performance reviews.

**Congratulations:
you've completed the book!**

APPENDIX A:
EXERCISE ANSWERS FOR CHAPTERS 1–4

(Below, we've omitted all the exercises where you prepared the first draft of your own work-related document.)

EXERCISE 1.2

It's difficult to determine the purpose for this email, but the revision on p. 9 is more clear. (Sorry for the trick question!)

EXERCISE 1.3

The purpose of this email is to persuade the reader to prepare meeting agendas.

EXERCISE 1.5

Email B has a clear main point.

EXERCISE 1.8

Just two of many ways you might reorganize the activities are by expense, or by whether you personally enjoy them.

EXERCISE 2.5

Here's one possible paragraph revision in list format.

> The task force found that the customer service representatives need training in how to respond to problems and complaints. <u>The members of the task force believe they need to address three primary areas of concern during the next six months:</u>
>
> - There is widespread unhappiness about the quality of food in the cafeteria, indicating the need to find another vendor.
> - They need additional study into ways to implement flexible hours without creating logistical problems.
> - Field representatives need newer tablets, which have not been included in this year's budget.

EXERCISE 2.6

Here's one possible paragraph revision in list format.

> To help us update our database, please review the enclosed listings and notify us of any changes. <u>Please take these steps:</u>
>
> 1. Proofread each listing and indicate any necessary corrections.
>
> 2. Enter the best address for clients to reach you, and verify that the telephone numbers and email addresses are correct.
>
> 3. Add a maximum of two lines of explanation to each listing, if you wish to.

EXERCISE 3.1

1. We <u>surveyed</u> the members.

2. Our manager <u>offered</u> to buy everyone coffee.

3. I believe this procedure will <u>improve</u> the way we file reports.

4. He called us <u>about</u> his recent insurance claim.

EXERCISE 3.2

1. The residents of the city are unhappy with the new regulations.

2. The subterranean garage is more secure than the old one.

3. Until last week, our group had the best record.

EXERCISE 3.3

1. The News Department is conducting the research project.

2. Please staple a copy of the approval to the request before you forward it to the Accounting Office.

3. I have attached the new design. I would appreciate it if you can review it and return it by March 15.

EXERCISE 3.4

Here are some possible revisions.

1. Last week we looked at a four-story building that might be big enough for our planned expansions and upgrades.

2. At the meeting, we will discuss the next conference, the move to the new building, and the new staff position, so please leave at least three hours in your schedule.

EXERCISE 3.5

1. prior to   before
2. subsequent to   after
3. utilize   use
4. supplemental   additional
5. heretofore   previously
6. commence   start
7. endeavor   try

EXERCISE 4.1

1. The sale doesn't start until next week, and <u>it's</u> not possible for us to offer you the special price until then.

2. <u>Too</u> many trees are being uprooted for the new development and not being replanted.

3. <u>There</u> seems to have been some confusion about the agenda for Friday's meeting.

4. Our department almost lost <u>its</u> certification during last week's evaluation.

5. Please let me know whether <u>you're</u> going to attend Barney's retirement party.

EXERCISE 4.2

1. the director's office
2. several days' backlog
3. the men's desks
4. anyone's wallet
5. RFP<u>s</u>
6. 19<u>80s</u>

EXERCISE 4.3

1. Your order should arrive by May 12th at the latest<u>:</u> our records indicate that it was shipped to your Denver office on May 4th.

   (The second idea directly explains the first idea.)

2. I'll start managing the XYZ project next month<u>;</u> I'm sure we'll need your help.

   (The second idea is not a direct explanation of the first idea.)

3. The consultant recommended that we put all of our procedure manuals online<u>;</u> she billed for three days of work last week.

   (The second idea is not directly related to the first idea.)

4. I am ready <u>to interview</u> five applicants, decide who is most qualified, and hire two people.

   ("I am ready to" could not become its own sentence with just a period after "to.")

APPENDIX B: THE WRITE IT WELL SERIES ON BUSINESS COMMUNICATION

Here's our full line of organizational- and career-development books on communication skills. They range from resume writing for job applicants to email for new hires to speaking and writing skills for managers.

- *Essential Grammar*: Brush up on grammar, punctuation, and usage details that help you project a professional image

- *Land the Job*: Tailor your resume and cover letter to a specific organization's hiring needs

- *Effective Email*: Improve the quality and reduce the quantity of your job-related email

- *Professional Writing Skills*: Plan, draft, and send any document at all to match any professional purpose (for readers with time for more detailed techniques than you find in *Writing at Work*)

- *Develop and Deliver Effective Presentations*: Plan, rehearse, and deliver a presentation on any professional topic

- *Reports, Proposals, and Procedures*: Draft multisection, high-stakes business documents

- *Writing Performance Reviews*: Keep performance documentation clear, specific, and appropriate for today's workplace

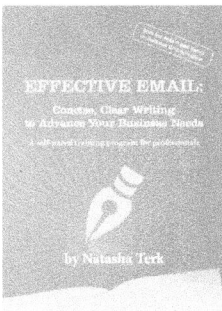

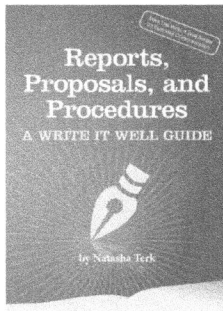

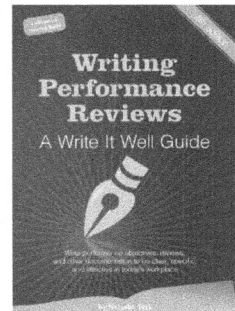

SCRATCH PAPER

SCRATCH PAPER